LET THE PUN
SHINE

FUN PUNS TO BRIGHTEN YOUR DAY

TEO ZIRINIS

DOG 'N' BONE

PUBLISHED IN 2019 BY DOG 'N' BONE BOOKS
AN IMPRINT OF RYLAND PETERS & SMALL LTD

20-21 JOCKEY'S FIELDS   341 E 116TH ST
LONDON WC1R 4BW   NEW YORK, NY 10029

WWW.RYLANDPETERS.COM

10 9 8 7 6 5 4 3 2 1

TEXT AND ILLUSTRATIONS ON PAGES 6-9, 11, AND 40 © TEO ZIRINIS 2019
DESIGN AND ALL OTHER ILLUSTRATIONS © DOG 'N' BONE BOOKS 2019

A CIP CATALOG RECORD FOR THIS BOOK IS AVAILABLE FROM
THE LIBRARY OF CONGRESS AND THE BRITISH LIBRARY.

ISBN: 978 1 912983 04 9

PRINTED IN CHINA

ILLUSTRATOR: TEO ZIRINIS

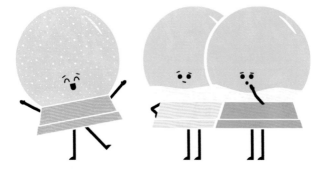

CONTENTS

INTRODUCTION

PUNS ARE LIKE BRUSSELS SPROUTS. YOU EITHER LOVE THEM OR HATE THEM. I LOVE PUNS, BUT HATE BRUSSELS SPROUTS. THIS IS WHY THE FORMER HAVE ALWAYS BEEN A GREAT SOURCE OF INSPIRATION FOR MY DRAWINGS, AND THE LATTER HAVE NOT. UNLIKE BRUSSELS SPROUTS, PUNS HAVE NEVER FAILED TO PUT A SMILE ON MY FACE AND LIGHTEN UP MY MOOD.

COMING UP WITH A RANDOM, SILLY PUN, PROUDLY SHARING IT WITH THE WORLD, AND APOLOGIZING FOR IT—AS TO FOLLOW PROPER ETIQUETTE—IS SOMETHING THAT I'LL NEVER TIRE OF. ON THE OTHER HAND, I GET TIRED OF BRUSSELS SPROUTS VERY QUICKLY.

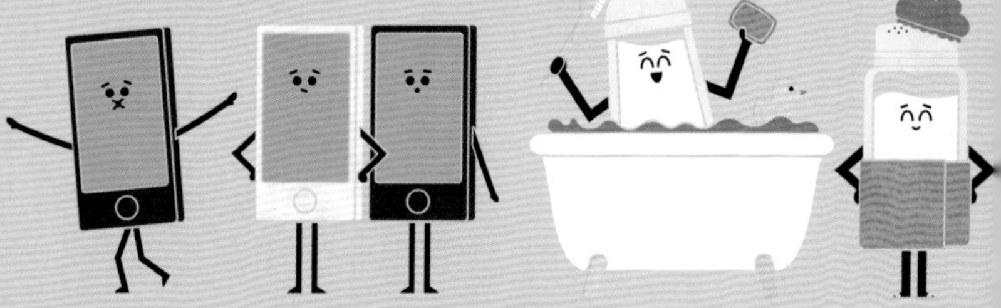

I GUESS WHAT I'M TRYING TO SAY IS...
IF YOU ENJOY PUNS, THEN I THINK YOU'LL FIND THIS BOOK TO YOUR LIKING.

IF YOU HATE BRUSSELS SPROUTS, HIGH FIVE!

NOW PUT ON YOUR PUNGLASSES AND ENJOY THE PUNSHINE. I APOLOGIZE IN ADVANCE.

:)

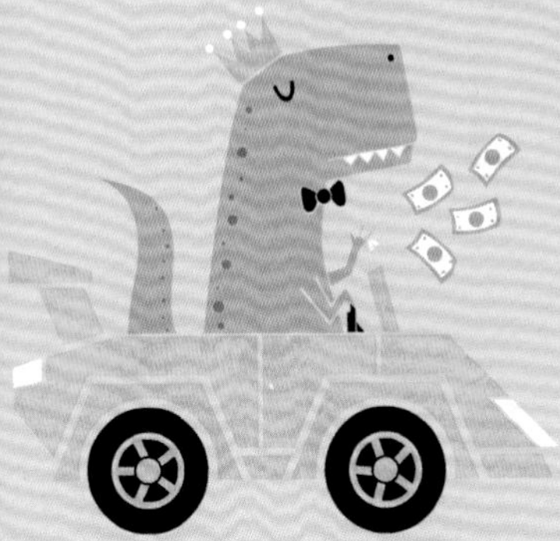

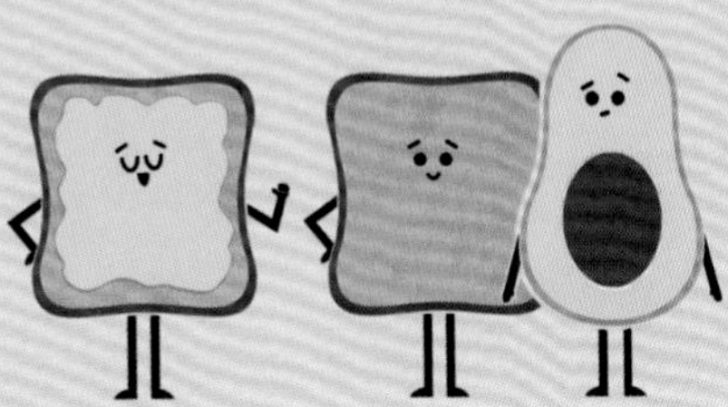

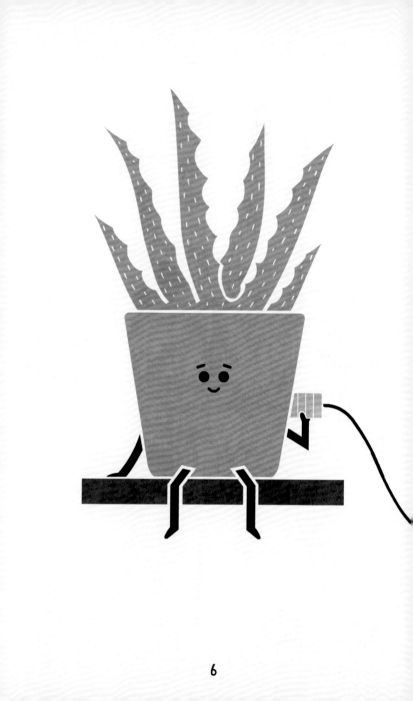

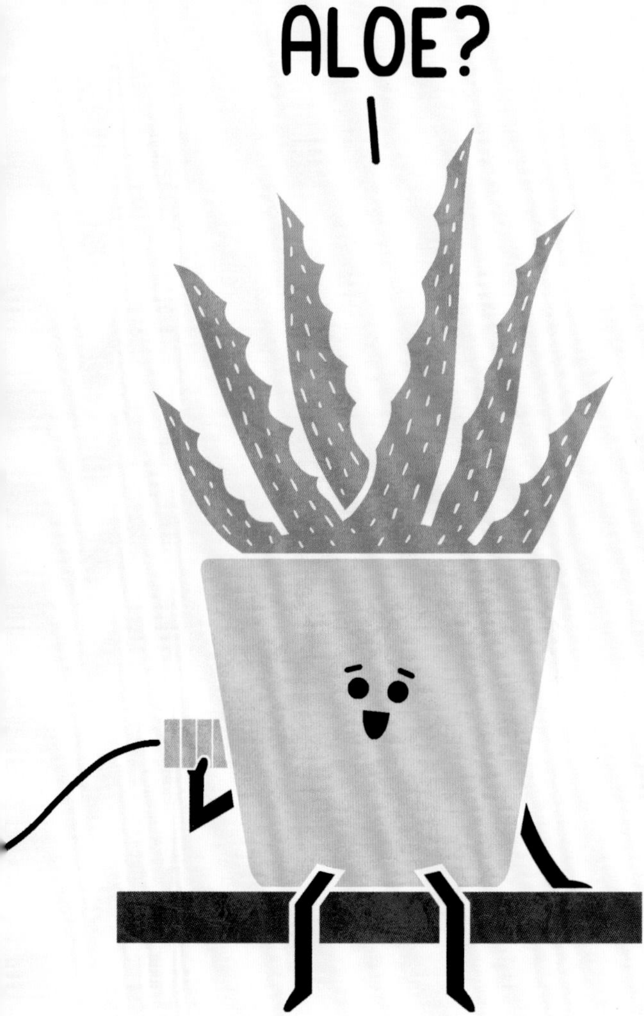
ALOE?

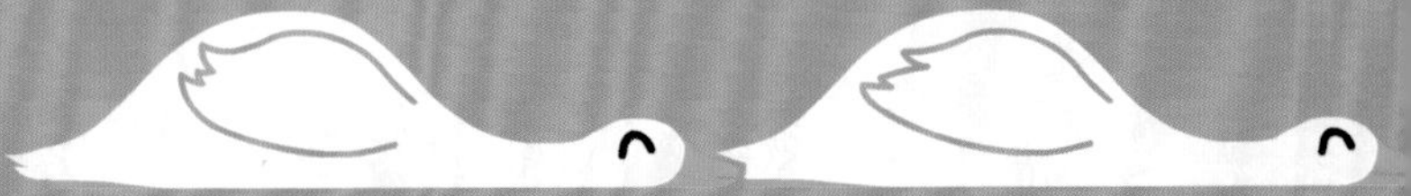

GOOSE BUMPS

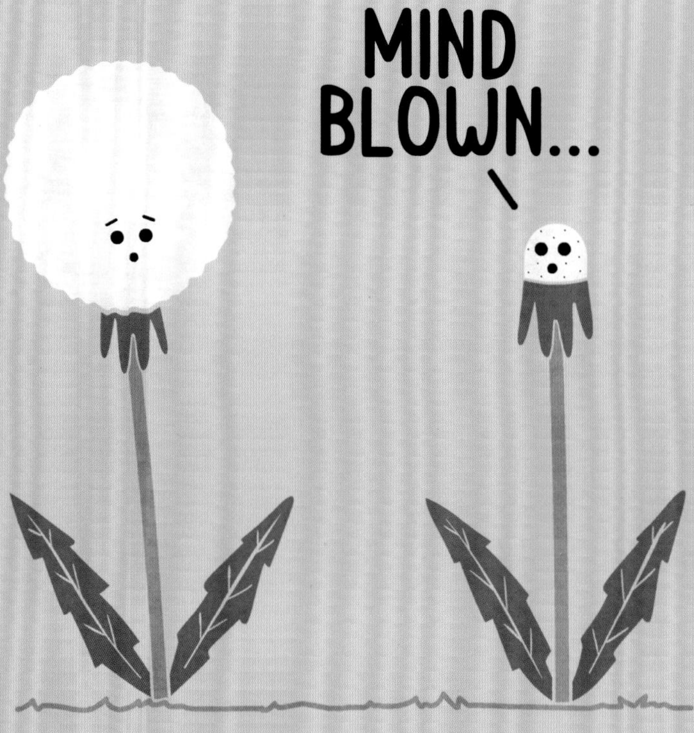
MIND BLOWN...

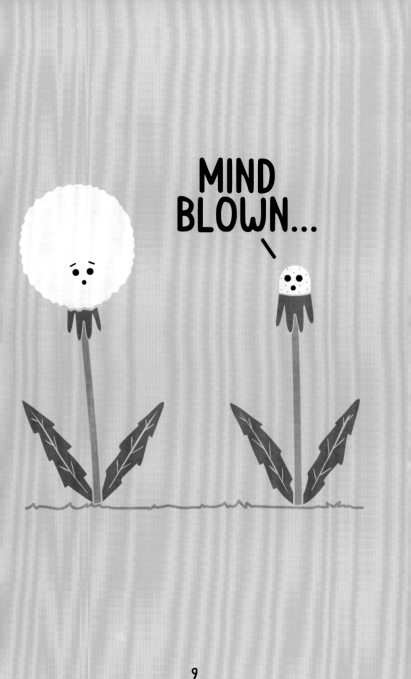

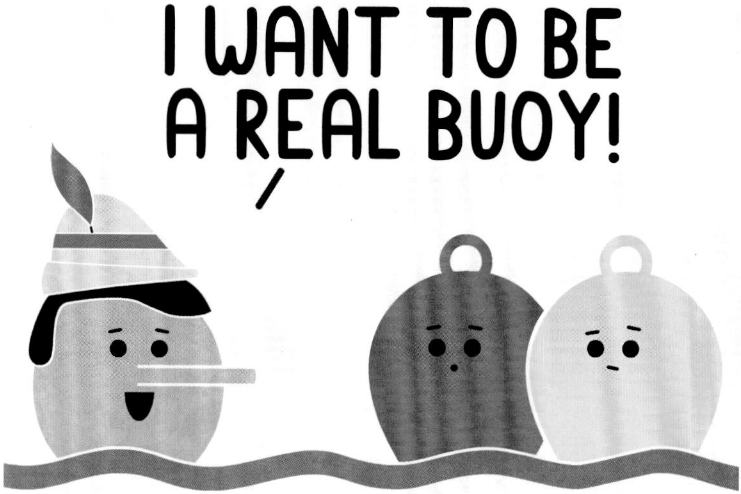
I WANT TO BE A REAL BUOY!

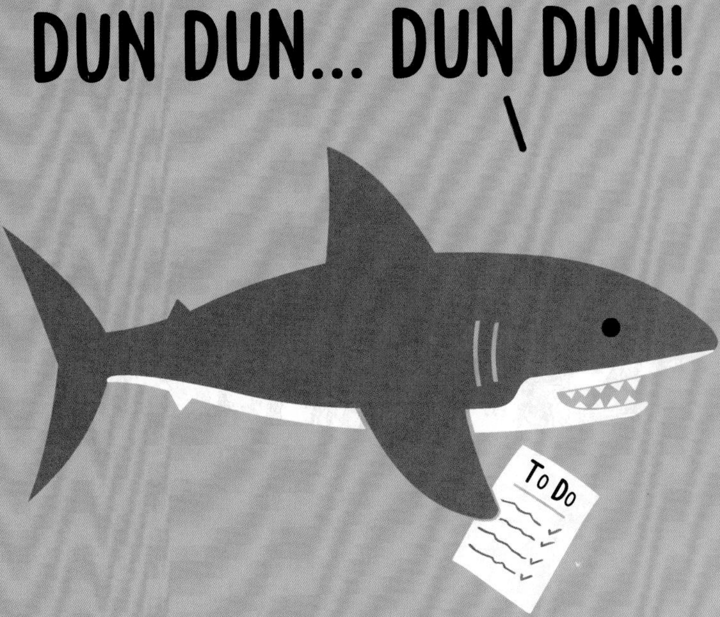
DUN DUN... DUN DUN!
To Do

WHISKI

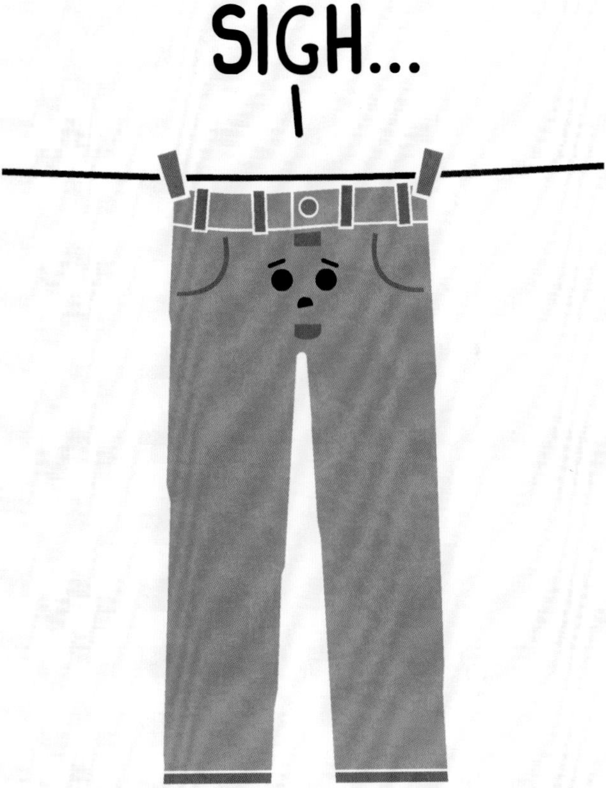
SIGH...

BLUE JEANS

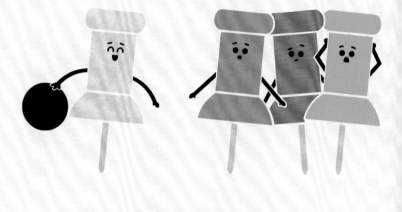

BOWLING PIN

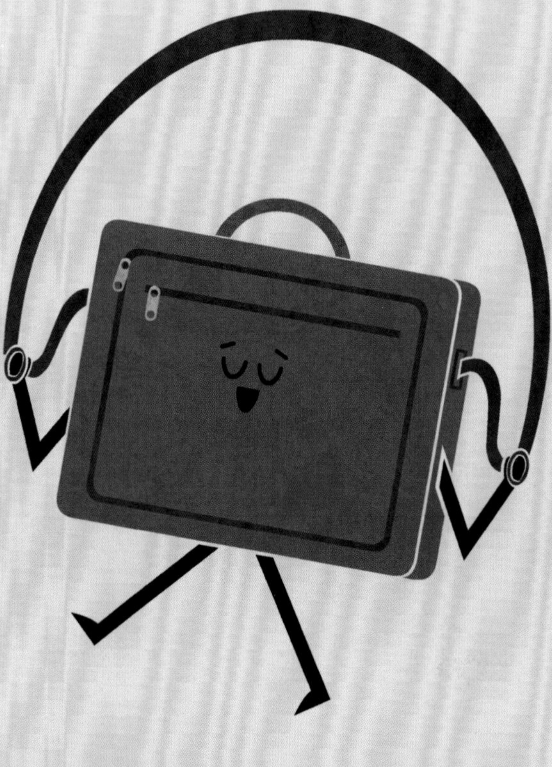

SKIPPING WORK

FIT AS A FIDDLE

TOOL BOX

I-BALLS

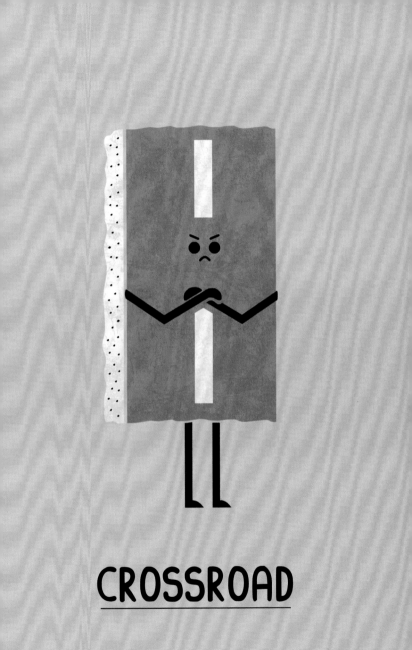

CROSSROAD

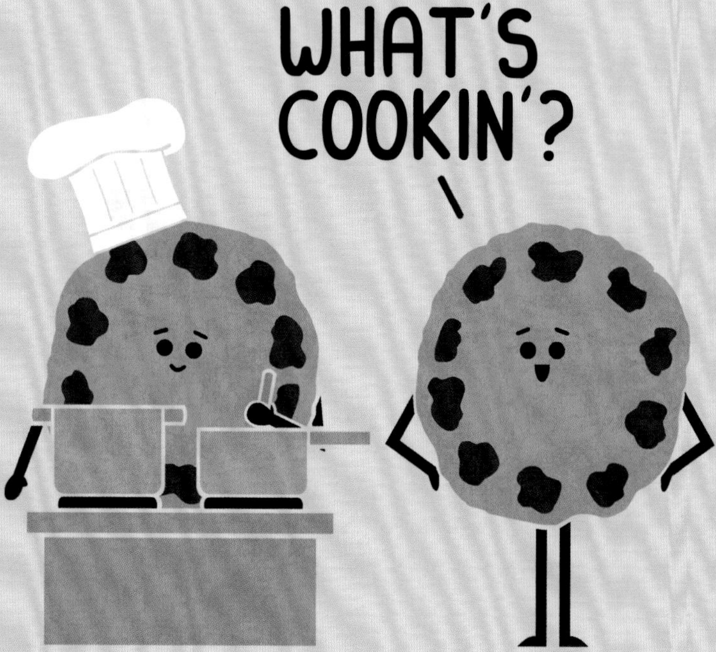
WHAT'S COOKIN'?

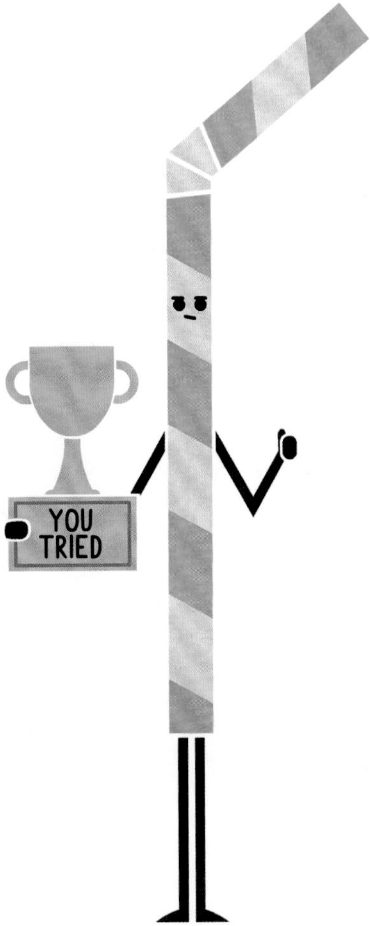
YOU
TRIED

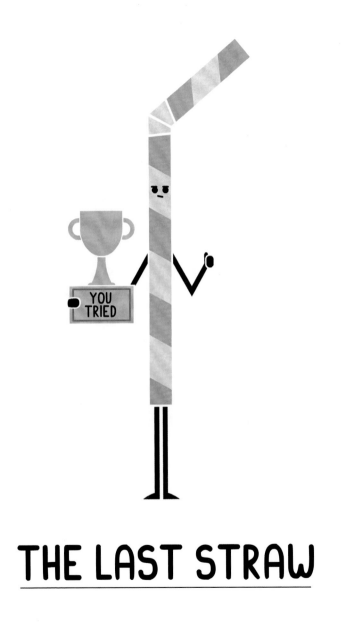

THE LAST STRAW

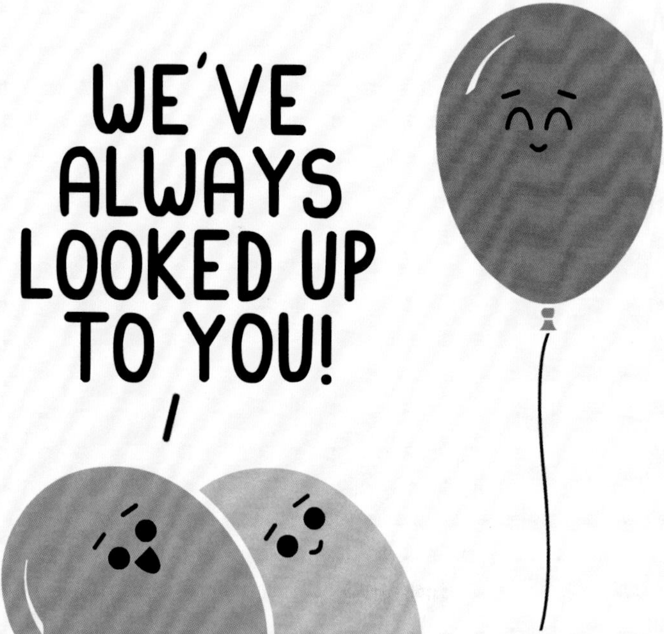
WE'VE ALWAYS LOOKED UP TO YOU!

CRASHED SAUCER

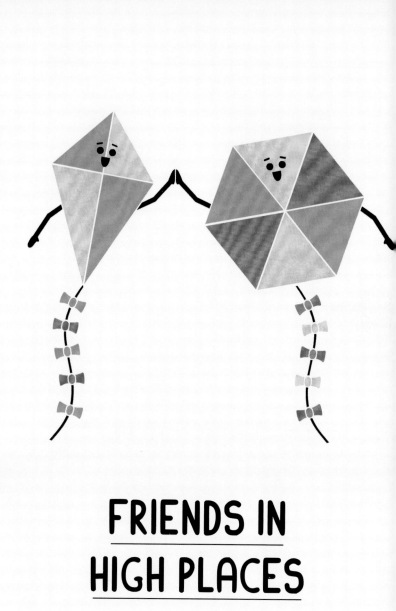

FRIENDS IN
HIGH PLACES

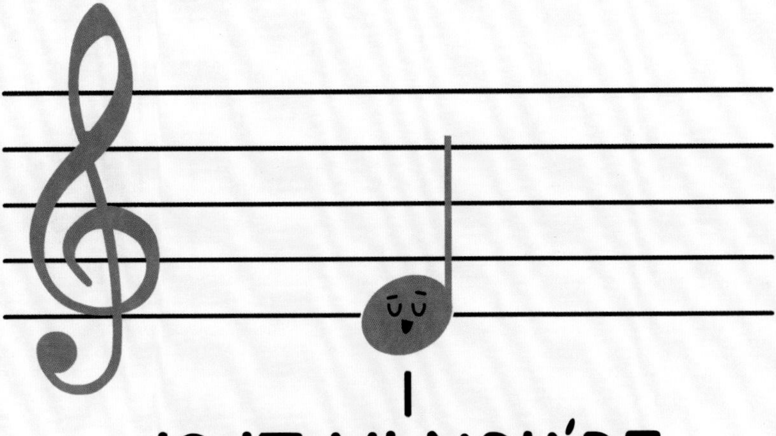

IS IT MI YOU'RE LOOKING FOR?

VI-PEA

I'M GONNA MAKE A SCENE!

LITTERATURE

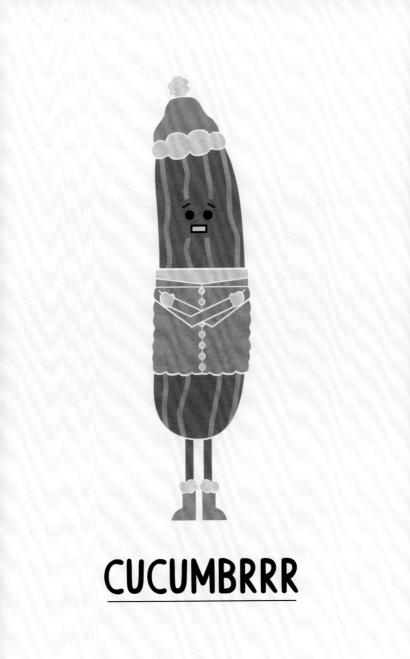

CUCUMBRRR

PHOTOCOPIER

Z

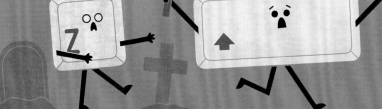

GRAVEYARD SHIFT

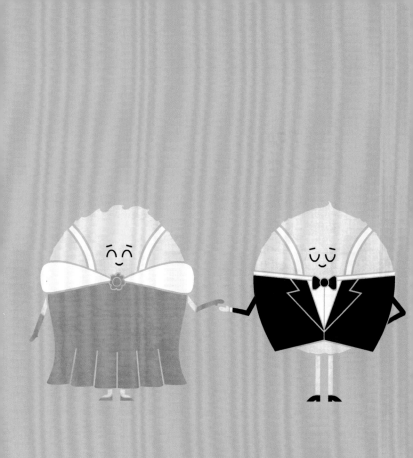

TENNIS BALL

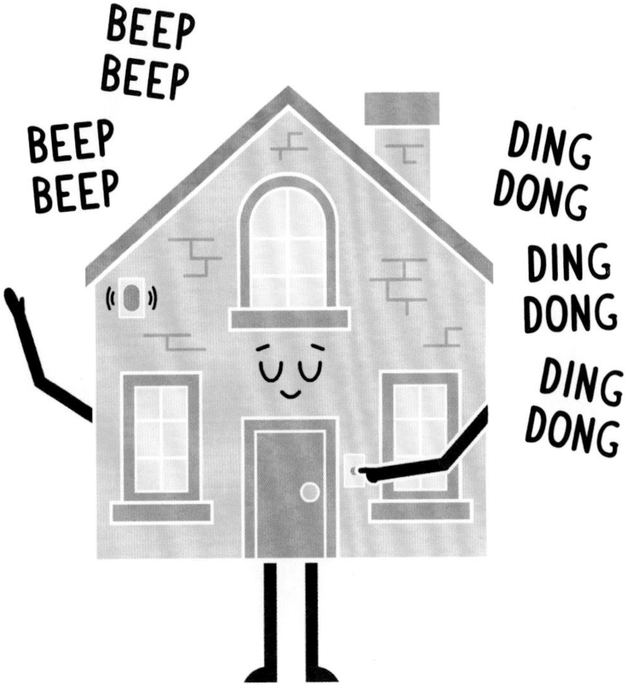
BEEP
BEEP
BEEP
BEEP
DING
DONG
DING
DONG
DING
DONG

HOUSE MUSIC

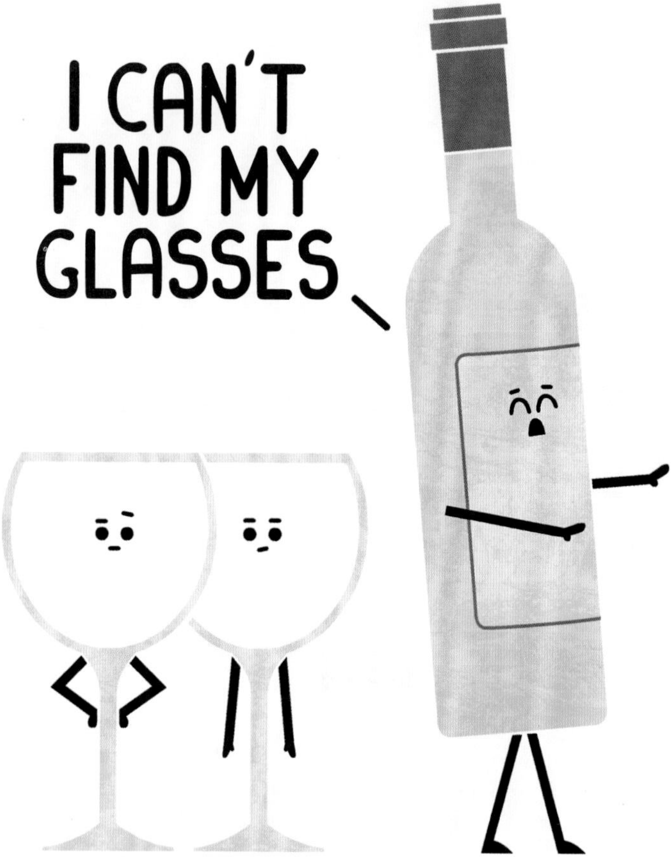
I CAN'T
FIND MY
GLASSES

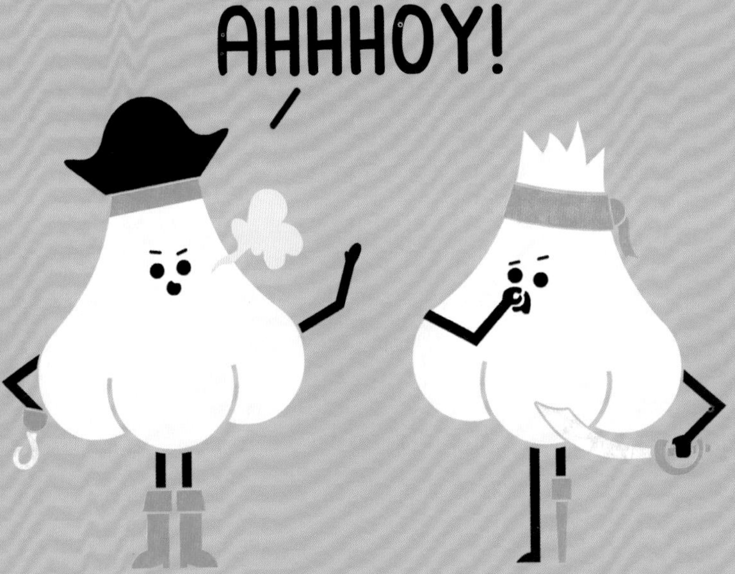
AHHHOY!

GARRRLIC

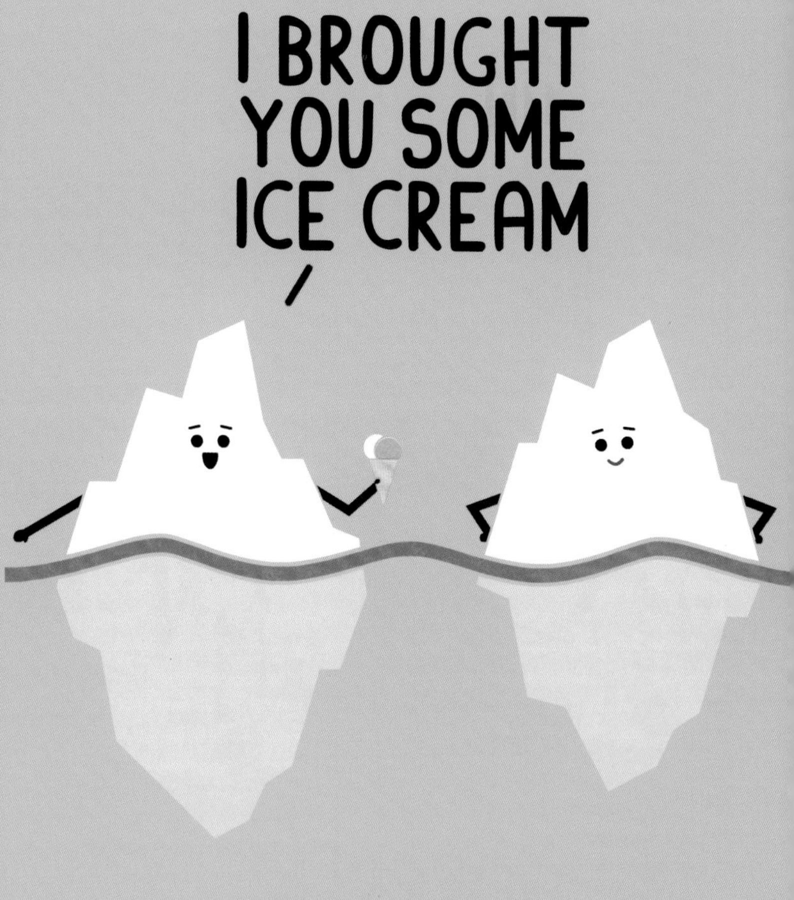

NICEBERG

I WANT TO SHARE MY FORTUNE WITH YOU! CAN I HAVE YOUR CARD DETAILS?

PHISHING BOAT

SHOW BEESNESS

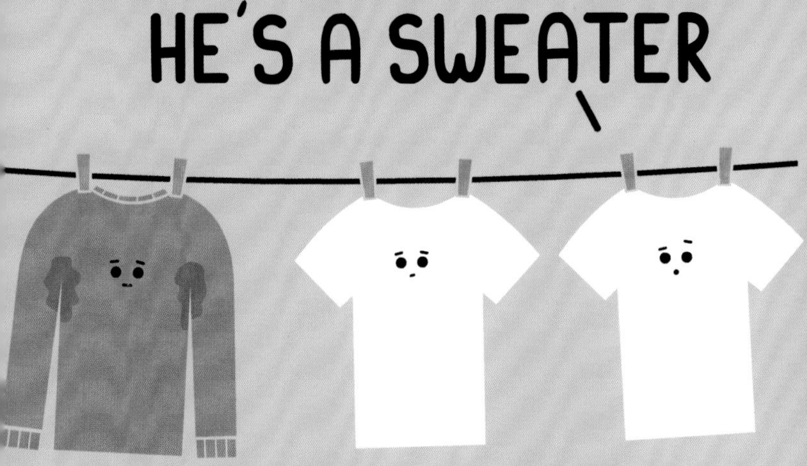
HE'S A SWEATER

SHE'S BRAINSTORMING...

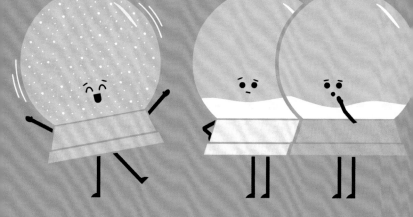

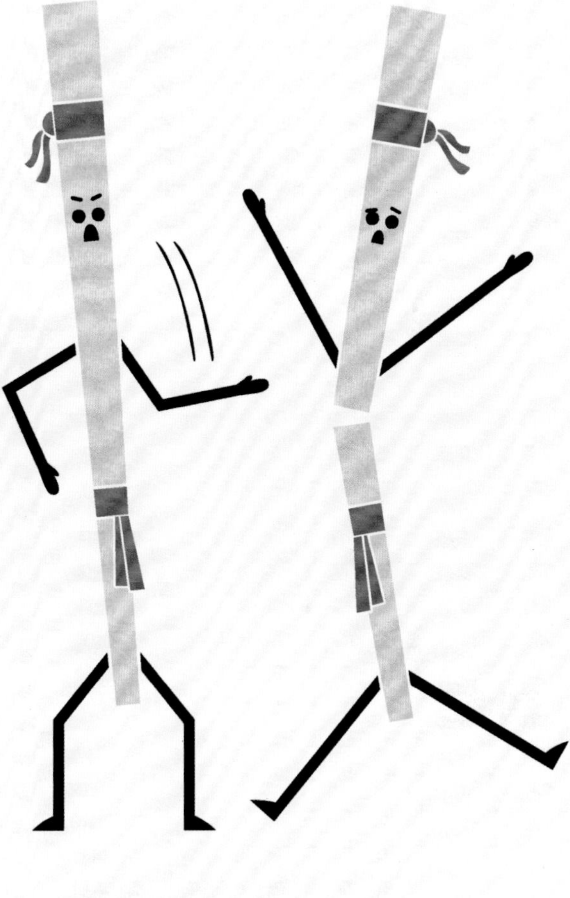

CHOPSTICK

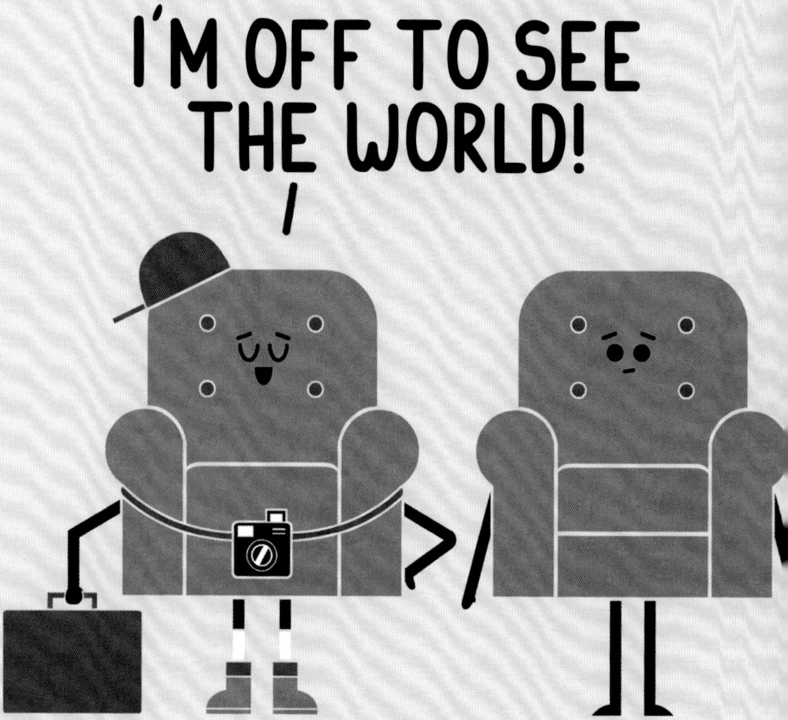
I'M OFF TO SEE THE WORLD!

ARMCHAIR TRAVELLER

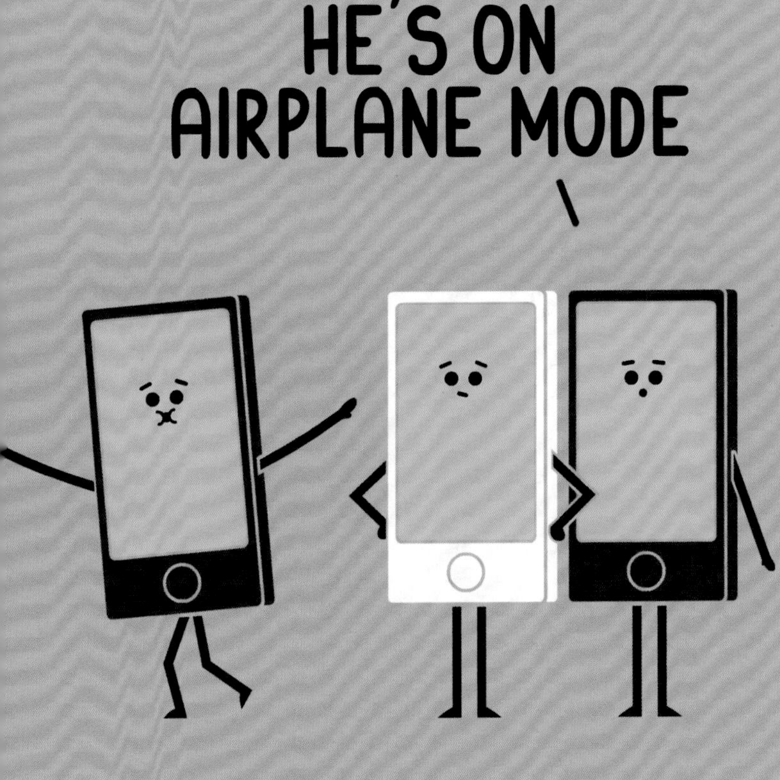
HE'S ON AIRPLANE MODE

LIFE IS PAIN

I

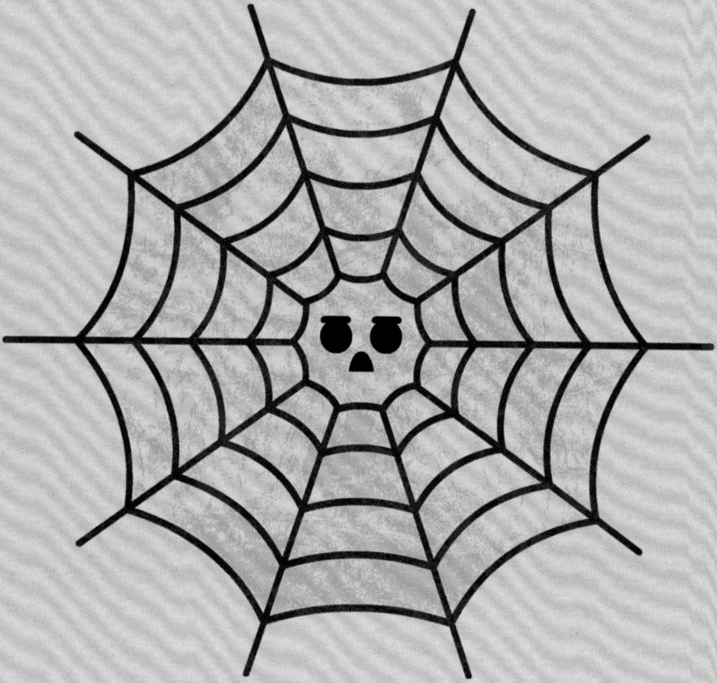

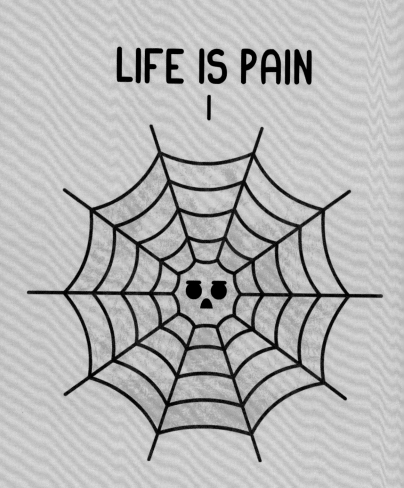

THE DARK WEB

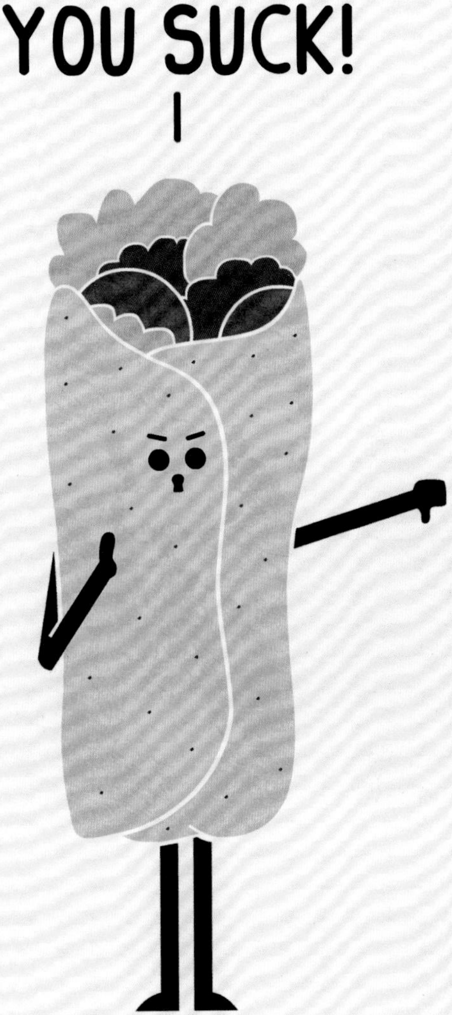

YOU SUCK!

BOORITO

RUDITÉS

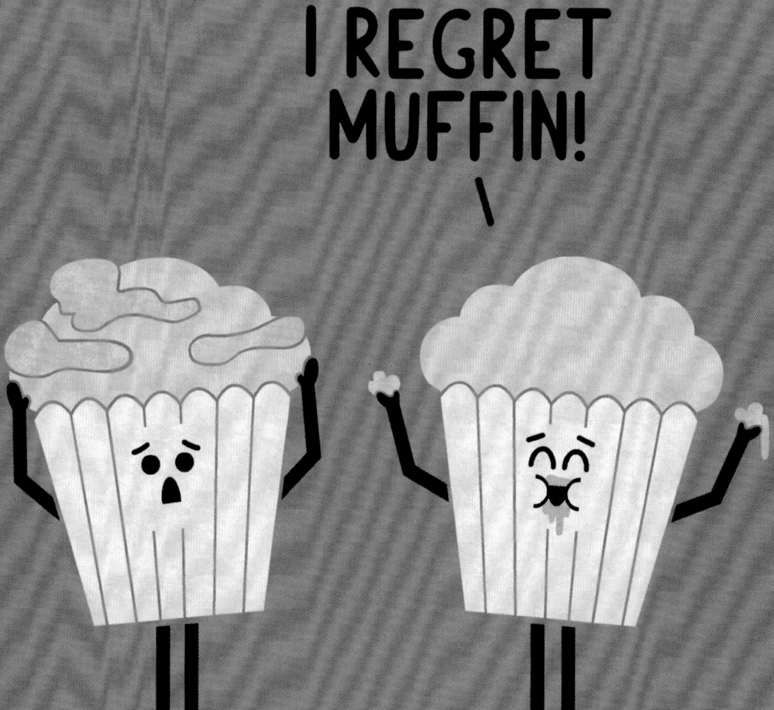
I REGRET
MUFFIN!

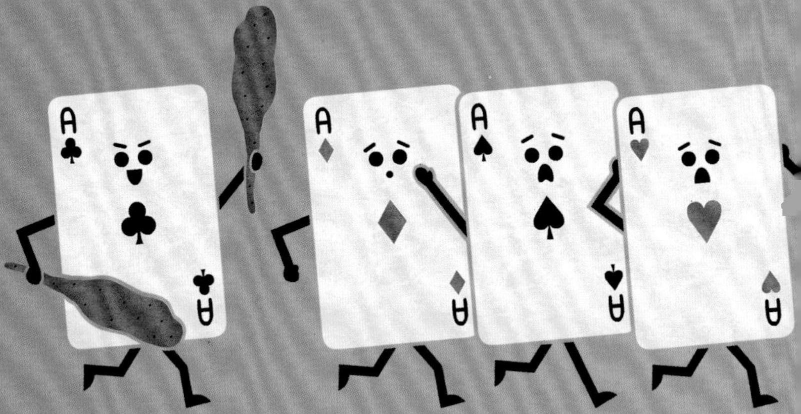
A
A
A
A

ACE OF CLUBS

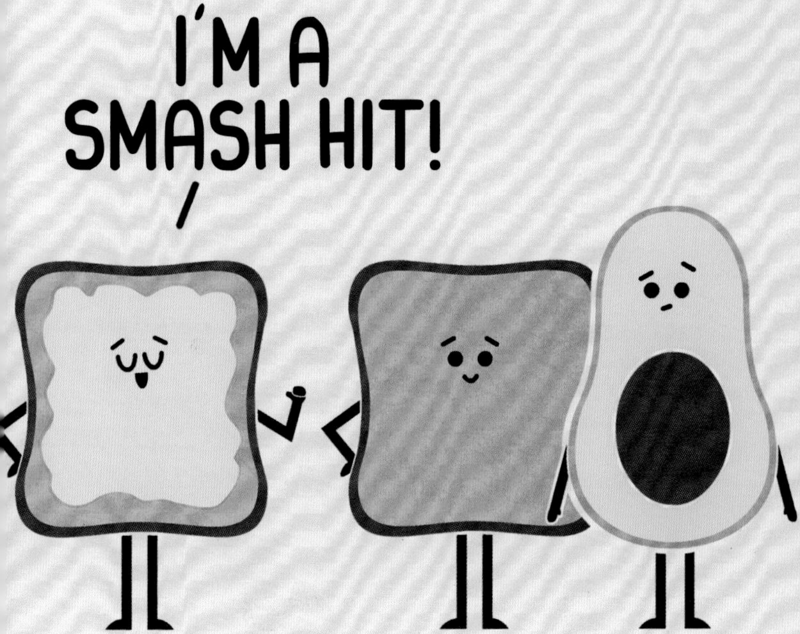
I'M A SMASH HIT!

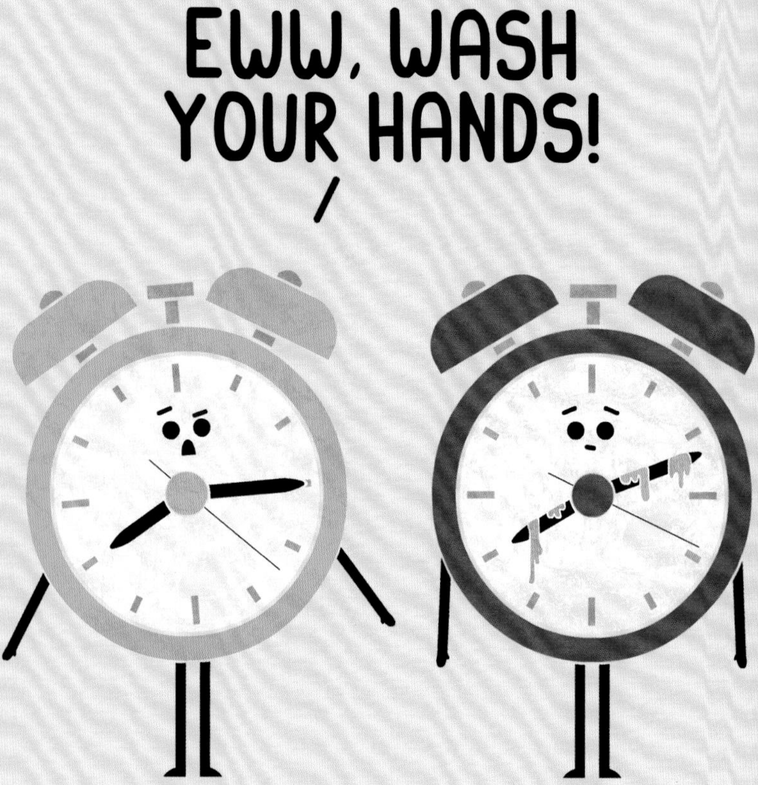
EWW, WASH YOUR HANDS!

BATH SALTS

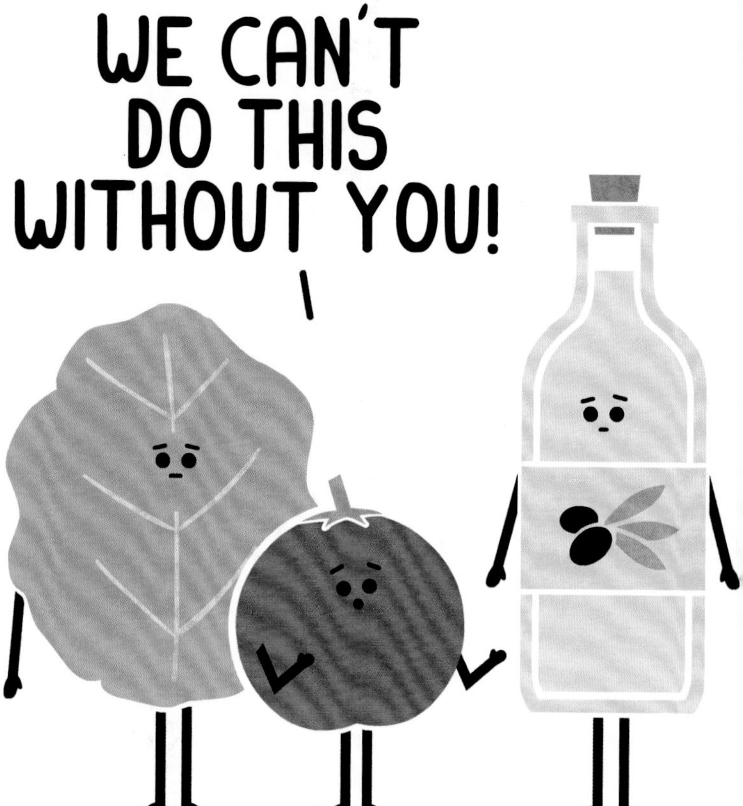
WE CAN'T DO THIS WITHOUT YOU!

ESSENTIAL OIL

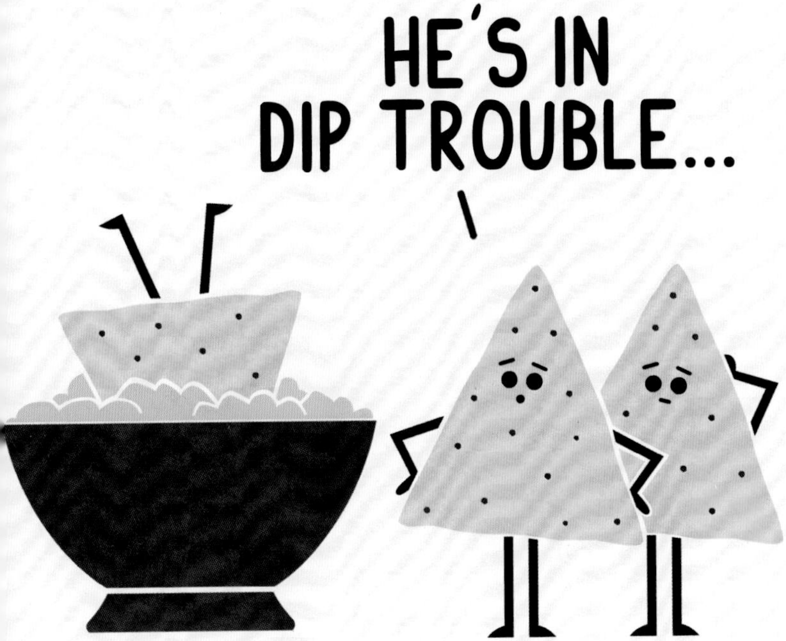
HE'S IN
DIP TROUBLE...

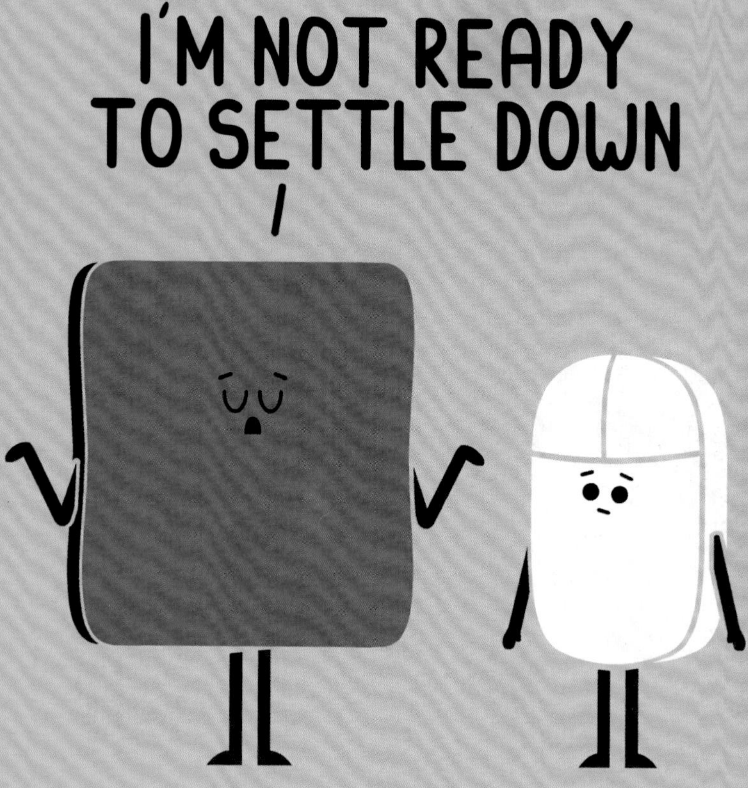

BACHELOR PAD

REXTRAVAGANT

MELTDOWN ALERT!

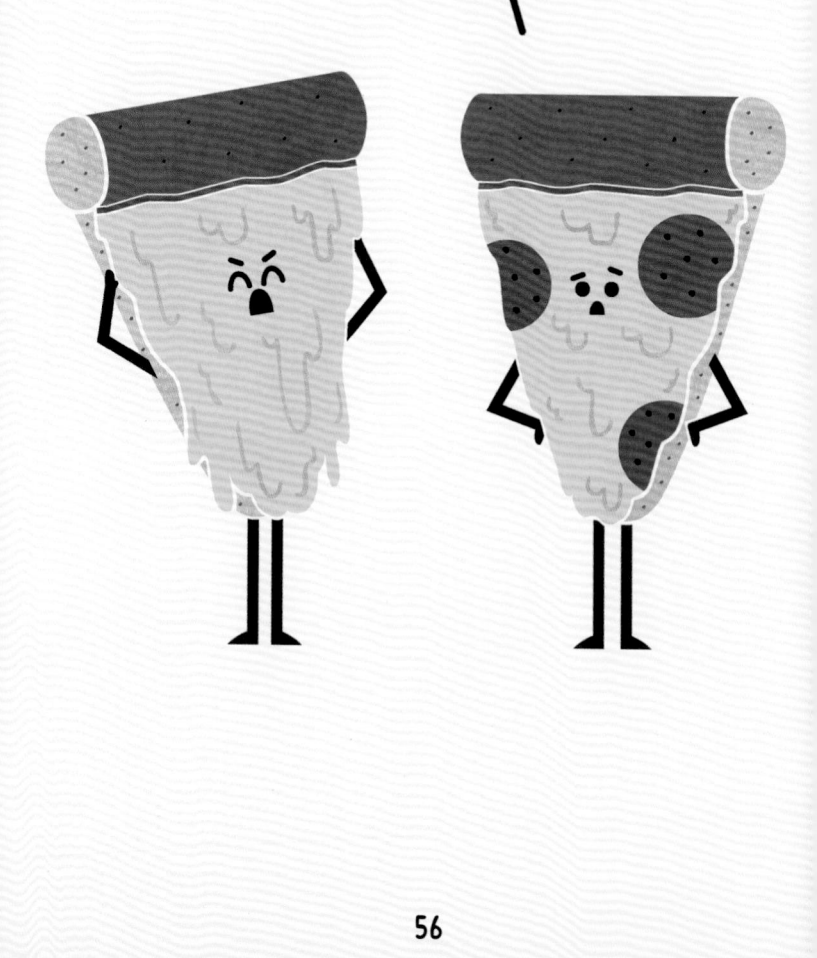

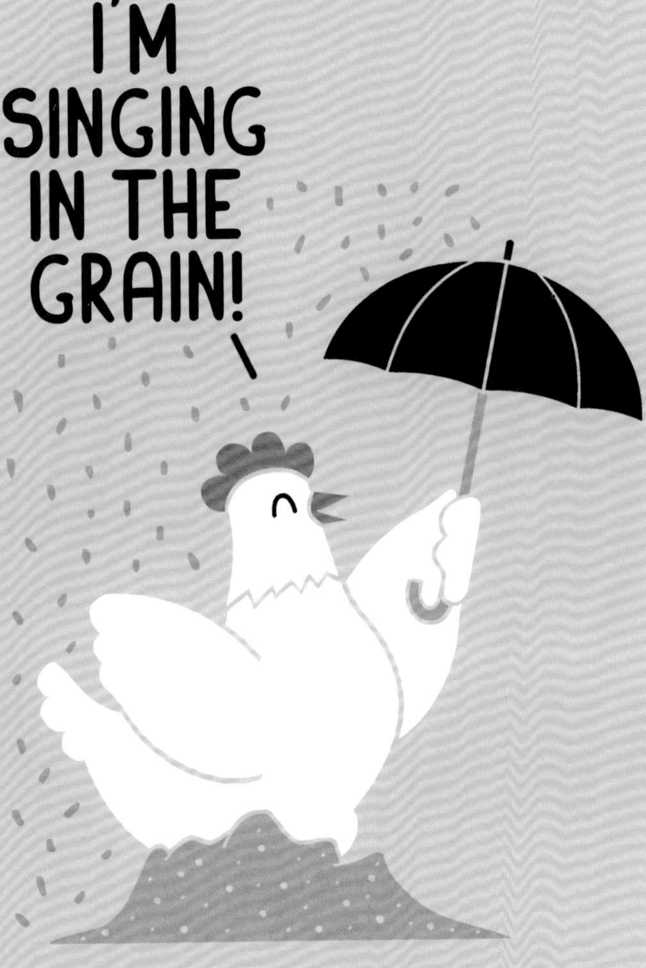
I'M SINGING IN THE GRAIN!

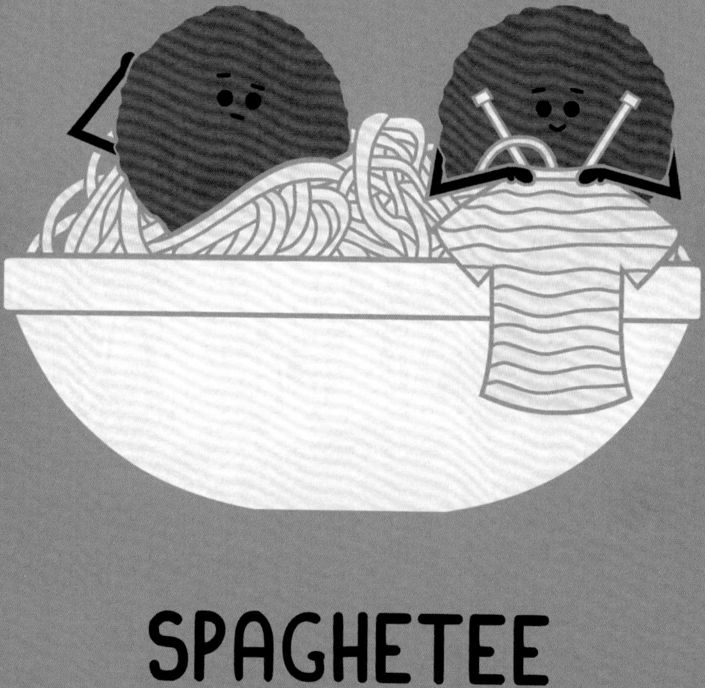

SPAGHETEE

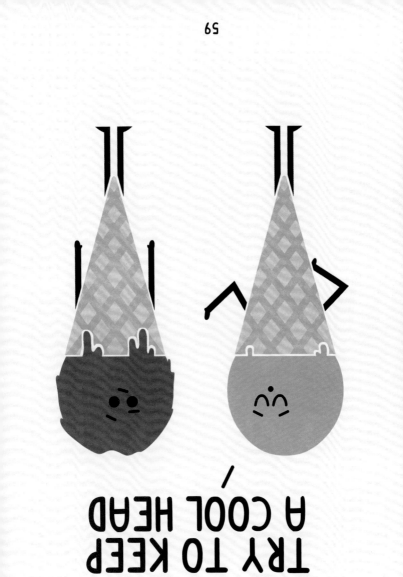

TRY TO KEEP
A COOL HEAD

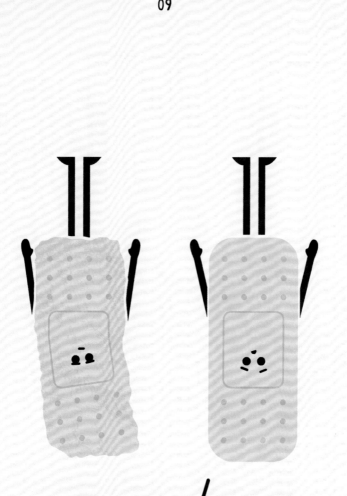

ROUGH PATCH?

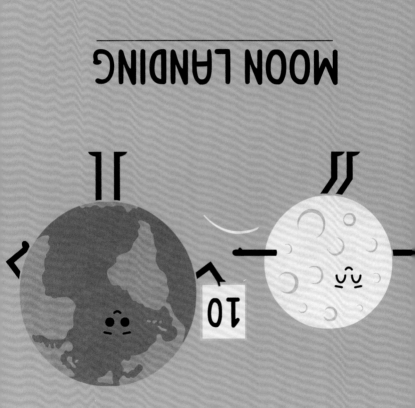

MOON LANDING

NAPPETIZERS

ZZZ

ZZZZ

YOU'RE FIRED!

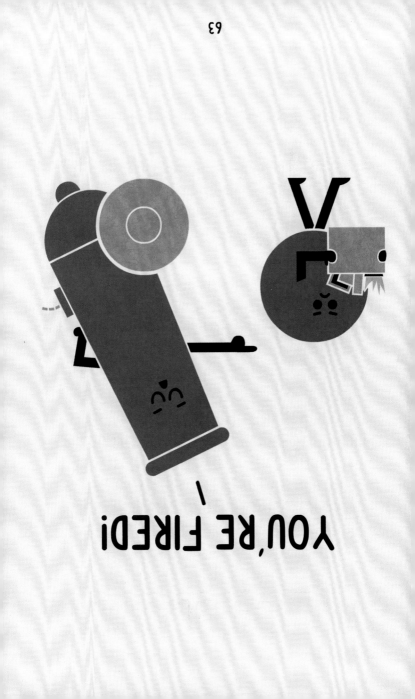

ACKNOWLEDGEMENTS

I WOULD LIKE TO THANK MY WIFE FOR BEARING
WITH ME AND MY CONSTANT DAYDREAMING. I AM
FOREVER GRATEFUL FOR HER LOVE AND PATIENCE.
THANKS TO MY FAMILY FOR ENCOURAGING ME TO
PURSUE MY WACKY ASPIRATIONS. THEY WERE
PROBABLY WORRIED, BUT IT NEVER SHOWED.
AND BIG THANKS TO MY CAT FOR KEEPING
MY CHAIR WARM.

I WOULD ALSO LIKE TO THANK EVERYONE AT
DOG'N'BONE AND CICO BOOKS, ESPECIALLY PETE
JORGENSEN, FOR MAKING IT ALL HAPPEN.

LAST BUT NOT LEAST, MANY THANKS TO YOU
FOR READING THIS SILLY LITTLE BOOK.
I HOPE YOU HAD AS MUCH FUN READING
IT AS I HAD MAKING IT.